THE PÈRE MARQUETTE
LECTURE IN THEOLOGY
1997

'FAITH ADORING THE MYSTERY':
READING THE BIBLE WITH ST. EPHRAEM THE SYRIAN

SIDNEY H. GRIFFITH
CATHOLIC UNIVERSITY OF AMERICA

MARQUETTE
UNIVERSITY
PRESS

BR
65
. E636
G75
1997

Library of Congress Cataloguing-in-Publication Data

Griffith, Sidney Harrison.
  Faith adoring the mystery : reading the Bible with St.
Ephraem the Syrian / Sidney H. Griffith.
    p. cm. — (The Père Marquette lecture in theology ; 1997)
  Includes bibliographical references.
  ISBN 0-87462-577-7 (cloth)
  1. Ephraem, Syrus, Saint, 303-373.   I. Title.   II. Series.
BR65.E636G75 1997
230' .14—dc21   97-4683

Copyright © 1997
Marquette University Press
Milwaukee WI 53201-1881

Manufactured in the United States of America

Marquette University Press
MILWAUKEE

The Association of Jesuit University Presses

FOREWORD

The annual Père Marquette Lecture in Theology commemorates the missions and explorations of Père Jacques Marquette, S.J. (1637-75). The 1997 lecture is the twenty-eigth in the series begun in 1969 under the auspices of the Marquette University Department of Theology.

The Joseph A. Auchter Family Endowment Fund has endowed the lecture series. Joseph Auchter (1894-1986), a native of Milwaukee, was a banking and paper industry executive and a long-time supporter of education. The fund was established by his children as a memorial to him.

SIDNEY H. GRIFFITH, S.T.

The lecture for 1997 is given by Sidney H. Griffith, S.T. Fr. Griffith was born in 1938 in Gaithersburg, Maryland. After attending the Holy Trinity Mission Seminary, in Winchester, Virginia, he was ordained a priest (Missionary Servant of the Most Holy Trinity) in 1965. Fr. Griffith went on to receive his Licentiate in Theology from The Catholic University of America (CUA), in 1967; he received his Ph.D., in the area of Syriac and Mediæval Arabic, from CUA's Department of Semitic and Oriental Languages and Literatures in 1977. Fr. Griffith has taught at CUA since 1977; since 1984, he has been the director of CUA's Graduate

Program in Early Christian Studies. Fr. Griffith has been a fellow at the Institute for Advanced Studies, The Hebrew University of Jerusalem, as well as at the Dumbarton Oaks Center for Byzantine Studies. He has been president of both the Byzantine Studies Conference and the North American Patristic Society. Since 1986, Fr. Griffith has served as a member of the Catholic Delegation to the Eastern Orthodox/Roman Catholic Consultation. Fr. Griffith has published numerous works in the areas of Syriac Christianity and Christian Arabic. Fr. Griffith 1997 Père Marquette Lecture is entitled 'Faith Adoring the Mystery': Reading the Bible with St. Ephraem the Syrian and represents the recent work by scholars in the new project of the recovery of Syriac Christianity.

Scholarly interest in the Syriac-speaking Christianity of early Byzantine Syria and Sassanid Persia, aside from Biblical studies and the occasional intrepid explorer, is a relatively new phenomenon. There is the pioneering work of Arthur Voeoebus and Dom Edmund Beck in the 1940s, 50s, and 60s, but it is really with people such as Robert Murray and Sebastian Brock from the 1970s onward that excitement and interest began steadily to mount. Today the area is well on its way toward becoming the major field of patristic research, alongside of, and increasingly equal to the long-plowed acreage of the Greek and Latin Fathers.

Why this excitement? Three reasons should suffice. First, Syriac is a dialect of Aramaic, and Syriac Christianity thus represents a continuous Christian tradition whose idiom was governed by essentially the same language as was spoken by those fishermen, peasants, and tax collectors who gathered to hear the Lord Jesus preach in Roman Palestine, and who then went on to spread the new faith of the Messiah along the great trade routes of the Roman Orient. As a result, second, in the writings of an Ephrem Syrus (†373) or of an Aphrahat the Persian (fl. 340s), to name but two, readers discover themselves in touch with currents of Christian and pre-Christian, Jewish though that extend back into the Palestine of the first century AD and before. These currents, third, serve not only to shed light from new angles on Christian origins, including the books of the New Testament, but also on well known Greek and Latin Christian writers of the early centuries, and so on the formation of classic Christian doctrine, spirituality, and liturgy. It is, for example, now rightly felt to be impossible to account for Byzantine hymnology and monastic literature without recourse to Syrian Christian poetry and ascetic writings. To be sure, Syriac Christianity has an intrinsic value and appeal, a lyrical, poetic approach to theology which can appeal directly to the directly to the modern reader, but these ancient kinfolk of the better known world of the Western churches, Greek and Latin, also tell us valuable things about ourselves, about our own tradition(s), and the continuity of Christian experience. They reveal new facets, new ways of looking at ideas and customs that we had long thought perfectly familiar and thoroughly explained.

'Faith Adoring the Mystery':*

Reading the Bible with St. Ephraem the Syrian

Of all the writers of the Syriac-speaking churches in the patristic period, it is undoubtedly Ephraem, the deacon of Nisibis and Edessa, whose name is the most immediately recognized today among those who treasure the thought of the teachers of the east in the formative centuries of Christian thought. His lifetime spanned the first three quarters of the fourth century, arguably one of the most significant periods in the formulation of the classic statements of orthodox doctrine. What is more, well within the patristic period itself Ephraem's reputation as a holy man, poet, and theologian of note was widely proclaimed, well beyond the borders of his native Syria and the territories where Syriac was spoken. Within fifty years of his death, Palladius included a notice of Ephraem among the ascetic saints whose memory he celebrated in the *Lausiac History*.[1] Sozomen the historian celebrated Ephraem's memory as a popular ecclesiastical writer. He said of Ephraem's works, "They were translated into Greek during his life, …

and yet they preserve much of their original force
and power, so that his works are not less admired
when read in Greek than when read in Syriac."[2] Even
Saint Jerome claimed to recognize Ephraem's theological genius in a Greek translation he read of a
book by Ephraem on the Holy Spirit.[3] Later, in
Byzantium, so important a monastic figure as Theodore Studites held up the example of Ephraem for
the inspiration of his monks.[4] But surely the most
striking testimony to the Syrian saint's popularity in
patristic and medieval times is the fact that in the
Clavis Patrum Graecorum, the number of pages it
takes to list the works in Greek attributed to Ephraem
is second only to the number of pages devoted to
listing the works of John Chrysostom![5]

One notices immediately, however, that these
testimonies to Ephraem's great popularity all refer to
works in Greek. And in spite of the fact that Sozomen
testifies that Ephraem's works were translated into
Greek during the Syrian's lifetime, one of the effects
of the modern recovery of his genuine works in
Syriac is that scholars have come to recognize that for
the most part there is only a small relationship
between the writers whom we may for convenience
call 'Ephraem Graecus' and 'Ephraem Syrus.'[6] What
is more, in the biographical tradition, an examina-
tion of the Greek and Syriac sources reveals two very
different *personae,* which, for convenience, one might
style the 'icon of Ephraem Byzantinus' and the
'portrait of Ephraem Syrus.'[7] They depict saints of
very different character. The fact of the matter is that
with the modern publication of the genuine Syriac
works of Ephraem it becomes clear that for centuries

in the Graeco-Latin world, admirers had created an image of the Syrian holy man that suited their own ideas about the ancient paragons of monastic sanctity, but that they had little or no notion of the real Ephraem and his works.[8] It is one of the credits of modern scholarship to have recovered a view of Ephraem that seems to correspond to the facts. All his life he was never a monk, but he was a bishop's man, a 'single' person in God's service,[9] a minister in the local churches of Nisibis and Edessa, a deacon who was also a teacher, a poet, who was also one of the most insightful exegetes of the Bible in the fourth century.

II

Ephraem's works in Syriac first came to the attention of readers in the west in a substantial way with the publication in the seventeenth century of the six-volume Roman edition of works attributed to him in Greek, Syriac, and Latin; the Syriac works, with Latin translations, are included in volumes IV to VI. They are largely the work of Étienne Awad Assemani (1709-1782) and Pierre Mobarak, S.J. (1660-1742), Maronite scholars who worked in close association with J. S. Assemani (1687-1768) and others in the Maronite College in Rome and the Vatican Library.[10] While later scholars have sometimes been scathing in their comments about the quality of the edition, the fact remains that for all practical purposes it offered the first glimpse of the genuine works of Ephraem the Syrian to Europeans who had hitherto known only the works of Ephraem

Graecus and their numerous translations and adap-
tations in other languages.

In subsequent years, beginning in the nine-
teenth century, and reaching well into the twentieth
century, scholars in England, Belgium, and other
parts of Europe, making use of the numerous manuscripts recently acquired in the west, made major
strides in publishing the rest of the Syriac works
attributed to Ephraem.[11] By the 1920's his theological reputation in Rome had grown to the point that
Pope Benedict XV proclaimed St. Ephraem a doctor
of the Universal Church, in an encyclical letter
issued on 5 October 1920.[12] But already it was
becoming clear that the first publications of
Ephraem's Syriac works left much to be desired in
terms of the quality of the editions of the texts; many
of them were not based on the best available manuscripts, and the work of many of the editors did not
satisfy the requirements of truly critical editions. To
remedy this situation, Dom Edmund Beck, O.S.B.
(1902-1991) began in 1955, and continued for the
next quarter century, to publish critical editions and
German translations of the genuine, Syriac works of
Ephraem in the Louvain series *Corpus Scriptorum
Christianorum Orientalium.*[13] The hallmark of Beck's
method was the choice of the best, earliest manuscripts to serve as the base manuscripts for his
editions, and the practice of displaying the texts on
the page in a way that highlights the literary form of
each piece. While Beck has not been alone in the task
of editing and publishing Ephraem's works in the
twentieth century, the sheer volume of his output in
this enterprise makes his name almost synonymous

with the production as it were of the 'complete works' of Ephraem Syrus.

The publication of the Syriac works of Ephraem has been accompanied by a crescendo in the number of studies devoted to them, and to his life and thought more generally.[14] The effect of all this attention has been gradually to bring Ephraem into the mainstream of modern patristic scholarship, although one can even now consult the index of too many studies of early Christian thought in areas on which he wrote extensively and still not find a mention of his name.[15] It is also interesting to observe the changes in the scholarly estimation of Ephraem's writing in the English-speaking world of the twentieth century.[16] Early on in the English-speaking world, F. C. Burkitt wrote that "Ephraim is extraordinarily prolix, he repeats himself again and again, and for all the immense mass of material there seems very little to take hold of. His style is as allusive and unnatural as if the thought was really deep and subtle, and yet when the thought is unraveled, it is generally commonplace.... Judged by any canons that we apply to religious literature, it is poor stuff."[17] More recently, J. B. Segal echoed the same sentiment. While admitting that Ephraem was a master of Syriac style, Segal went on to say that "his work, it must be confessed, shows little profundity or originality of thought, and his metaphors are laboured. His poems are turgid, humourless, and repetitive."[18] But in stark contrast to these negative judgments, Robert Murray has described Ephraem "as the greatest poet of the patristic age and, perhaps, the only theologian-poet to rank beside Dante."[19]

And now, as if in testimony to Murray's judgment, the composer/singer, John Tavener, has set several of Ephraem's stanzas in English translation to music and has issued a CD featuring them in performance.[20] Generally, it seems, the closer one studies Ephraem's works, and the more familiar the reader is with the text of the Bible, the more prepared one is to concede the genius not only of his language, but of his exegetical insights.

III

In the Syriac tradition, Ephraem is remembered as a teacher, and as an interpreter of the scriptures. Jacob of Sarug (c. 451-521), a Syriac writer whose literary reputation is second only to that of Ephraem himself, wrote a verse homily on "the holy man, Mar Ephraem, the teacher (*malpānâ*)," in which he presents Ephraem as a skilled preacher and composer of doctrinal hymns carefully wrought to commend right teaching and to refute error. Jacob celebrates Ephraem as:

A marvelous rhetor, who surpassed the Greeks in declamation;
    who could include a thousand subjects in a single speech.
A divine citharist; he set his phrases to verse, to make joyful
    sound in mighty wonder.[21]

In the seventh century Pseudo-Barḥabhabbâ (d. before 650), the historian of the schools of Edessa and Nisibis, echoed Jacob of Serugh's celebration of Ephraem's pedagogical talents when he accorded him the anachronistic title of 'Interpreter' (*mpashshqānâ*). In seventh century usage this title would identify him as the local church's chief biblical exegete, and the master of his city's school of religious education.[22] In fact, Pseudo-Barhadbshabbâ says that Jacob of Nisibis (d. 337/8) put Ephraem into a position in Nisibis comparable to that which bishop Alexander of Alexandria gave the young deacon Athanasius in his own city after the council of Nicea. And Pseudo-Barhadbshabbâ goes on to say that in later years in the Church of the East, before the works of Theodore of Mopsuestia (c. 350-428) had been translated into Syriac, the current 'Interpreter' at the school of Nisibis was still passing on "the traditions of Mar Ephraem."[23] Clearly Pseudo-Barhadbshabbâ was claiming a patristic authority for Ephraem in the Syriac-speaking community comparable to that of Athanasius in the Byzantine church.

It is customary to reckon the year 306 as the year of Ephraem's birth. When he reached his majority, he came into the service of bishop Jacob of Nisibis (c. 308-338), and he remained in the episcopal service of Nisibis through the tenure of the next three bishops, Babū (d. 346), Vologeses (d. 361), and Abraham (d. 363). Ephraem's diocesan service, therefore, lasted some forty years until the day in the reign of bishop Abraham, in the year 363, when he and other refugees left Nisibis on the occasion of her surrender to the Persians as part of the agreement Emperor Jovian (363-364) made after his predecessor Julian had met his death deep in Persian territory.[24] After the surrender of Nisibis, and his flight from the city westward, Ephraem came eventually to Edessa; there he entered the service of bishop Barses

(361-371), whom the Arianizing Emperor Valens (364-378) translated to the lesser see of Ḥarrān in 371.[25] Two years later —on 9 June 373, according to the *Chronicle of Edessa*—Ephraem died.[26]

Ephraem's lengthy bibliography of hymns, homilies, and biblical commentary testifies to the pastoral work he actually did in the service of his bishops. He was a teacher, a preacher, a biblical exegete, a theologian-poet whose discourse was Aramaic to the core. In his own idiom he commended to his flock what one now recognizes to be the orthodox faith of Nicaea, along with an unswerving loyalty to the Roman Empire.[27] His style of religious discourse was not academic; it was deeply contemplative, based on a close reading of the scriptures, with an eye to the telling mystic symbol (*râzâ*) or 'type' in terms of which God chose to make revelations to the church. In the context of the fourth century, in the 'Church of the Empire,' Ephraem's style of thought was archaic in the etymological sense of the word - it issued from the well-spring of what, in the monastic west, one would call *lectio divina*. The result was a colloquy with the Word of God, the mode of religious discourse that is prior to academic theology.

Everything we know about Ephraem's career in Nisibis and in Edessa, most of it from his own pen, suggests that he participated wholeheartedly in the pastoral work of the bishops whom he served. In his *Hymns against Heresies* he spoke of himself as a 'herdsman' (*ʿallānâ*), who by his writing helped tend the flock. In the last hymn of the collection he offered this prayer:

O Lord, may the works of your herdsman (ʿallānâ)
 not be defrauded;
I will not then have troubled your sheep,
 but as far as I was able,
I will have kept the wolves away from them,
 and I will have built, as far as I was capable,
Enclosures of hymns (madrāshê)
 for the lambs of your flock.[28]

In all probability Ephraem lived within a "fold
of herdsmen" (dayrâ dʿallānê), as he himself called
them, who worked together with the chief shepherd
(rāʿyâ) of the local Christians, and who, he said "had
rejoiced to see the succession of their ranks"[29] in the
service of Bishop Abraham of Nisibis. This dayrâ
would not have been a 'monastery', in our sense of
the word, and as the Syriac term itself would later be
interpreted.[30] But there is every reason nevertheless
to believe that Ephraem lived among his fellow
'herdsmen' as a single person (îhîdāyâ) in God's
service, a member of the so-called 'sons of the
covenant' (bnay qyāmâ), and perhaps as a deacon, as
the later tradition would insist.[31] Jacob of Sarug, in
his homily on Ephraem, 'the Teacher', characterized
him as "a godly Philosopher in his actions, who as he
was acting would also be teaching whoever would
listen to him."[32]

Ephraem's works in Syriac are almost all metrical compositions, or Kunstprosa, that is to say poetry,
in some sense of the word. It is true that he wrote
some works in more straightforward prose as well,
such as his commentaries on Genesis, Exodus and
the Diatessaron,[33] along with the collection of polemical texts which generally go under the title given

them by the editor of many of them, the so-called
Prose Refutations.[34] But there is no doubt that his
particular genius comes to full flower in the poetic
mêmrê and *madrāshê* that he penned, or the 'homilies' and 'hymns' as they are conventionally called in
the west.[35] Here we meet the quintessential Ephraem,
who expressed his thoughts in measured lines of
verse, usually in isosyllabic cola, which, in the
madrāshê, are arranged in stanzas, after each one of
which a response (*ʿunîtâ*) is usually repeated.[36]

It seems that Ephraem's hymns and homilies
had a liturgical setting;[37] St. Jerome says that in some
churches they were recited after the scripture lessons
in the divine liturgy.[38] The recitation was chanted to
the accompaniment of the lyre (*kennārâ*), on the
model of David, the Psalmist.[39] Indeed Ephraem's
Syriac poetry does bear a close, formal resemblance
to the prosody of the Hebrew Psalter, although the
closest literary analogue to the Syriac *madrāshê* in
other religious literatures is probably to be found in
the Hebrew *Piyyûtîm*, synagogue hymns which en-
joyed great popularity in Palestine from the eighth
century on. While these compositions are from a
later time and a different people, they do provide a
useful point of comparison. Two of the earliest
writers of them, Yannai and Qallir, employ literary
devices very similar to those regularly used by
Ephraem, and like him, they most often take their
themes from the Bible.[40] Similarly, Ephraem's poetry is in many ways not unlike that of the Byzantine
Kontakion. In fact, a good case can be made for the
suggestion that the most famous composer of
Kontakia, Romanos the Melode (d. after 555), who

was a native of Emesa in Syria, was actively influ-
enced by Ephraem's compositions.[41] All of these
works, Syriac, Hebrew and Greek, found their natural setting in liturgical circumstances, a fact that
underlines the dramatic character of their presentation. As for Ephraem's compositions in particular, it
is not unlikely that in them he was developing a style
of hymnody already at home in Syriac writing before
his time, the earlier examples of which have not
survived due to later considerations of orthodoxy,
and the overwhelming fame of Ephraem's own
works.[42]

Ephraem's *mêmrê* and *madrāshê*, which were
'occasional pieces', in the sense that he wrote them
for specific occasions, be they liturgical or didactic,
were gathered into collections by theme, and also by
melody, by his disciples and by later users and
transmitters of his compositions.[43] There is ample
evidence that in certain instances his work was even
expanded by others, the better to serve some more
immediate liturgical or memorial purpose.[44] And
sometimes verses and whole stanzas were rearranged
to suit new situations.[45] Some followers and imitators, now unknown by name, also wrote entire
compositions in Ephraem's name and included them
among his genuine works; others corrected or brought
up to date earlier, more surely genuine pieces.[46] All
this activity is testimony not only to Ephraem's
popularity and authority in the Syriac-speaking
churches, but also to the essentially public-service
character of much of his writing. He did not write
primarily tracts for scholars or meditation pieces for
monks, or even literary homilies intended for circu-

lation among the theological trend-setters. His texts were used for the most part by busy churchmen like himself, who had liturgies to celebrate or catechetical classes to teach. They often had no compunction about adapting his compositions to their own pressing purposes, or even about borrowing the authority of his name to commend a certain point of view in compositions of their own.

While it remains uncertain just how much Ephraem himself was involved in the collection of his works, it is clear that by the sixth century, the date of the earliest and best manuscripts, the compilations were essentially in the form in which we know them today. The evidence for the production of comprehensive volumes of Ephraem's hymns is found in remarks which occur in a number of manuscripts which transmit his works. But the principal document which has given scholars an insight into the final form taken by these volumes is Sinai Syriac MS 10, a text which in the judgment of André De Halleux may have its own roots as far back as the sixth century. From this source, which is meant to be a register of the forty-five melodies used in the whole collection of Ephraem's hymns, one learns of nine volumes of the author's collected *madrāshê*.[47]

One learns from Jacob of Sarug's homily on Ephraem, 'the Teacher', how important the correct performance of his *madrāshê* was for the busy deacon of Nisibis and Edessa. He reportedly spent time and energy rehearsing the groups who would perform them in church. And what is more, according to Jacob, he insisted that women take their rightful place in the church's choirs. On this subject, Jacob spoke of Ephraem as "a second Moses for women,"[48] and he addressed Ephraem as follows:

> In you, even our sisters were encouraged to sing [God's] praises, although it was not permissible for women to speak in church.[49]
>
> Your teaching opened the closed mouth of the daughters of Eve, and now the congregations of the glorious [church] resound with their voices.[50]
>
> It is a new sight that women would proclaim the Gospel, and now be called teachers in the churches.
>
> The aim of your teaching is the wholly new world, where, in the kingdom, men and women are equal.
>
> Your work put the two sexes together as two lyres, and you made men and women at once equal to sing [God's] praises.[51]

IV

The fact that so much of Ephraem's writing had a pastoral setting, a good portion of it even being produced as choral responses to the scripture lessons in the liturgy,[52] reminds one of the centrality of the Bible in all of his work. He was no less an exegete in his hymns and homilies than he was in the professedly biblical commentaries that have come down to us under his name. In fact, to hear Ephraem himself talk, his exegesis is to be found primarily in the hymns and homilies. At the beginning of his *Commentary on Genesis* he wrote:

> I had not wanted to write a commentary on the first book of Creation, lest we should now repeat what we had set down in the metrical homilies and hymns. Nevertheless,

compelled by the love of friends, we have written briefly
of those things of which we wrote at length in the metrical
homilies and in the hymns.[53]

The old *Editio Romana* of the works of Ephraem
contains commentaries attributed to him on most of
the books of the Old Testament *Peshitta*, and the
searches of subsequent scholars have uncovered even
more texts purporting to contain such commentaries.[54] While much scholarly work remains to be done
on these often fascinating compositions, it seems
clear enough that few of them can be authentic. In
fact, only the commentaries on Genesis and Exodus
are generally considered by modern scholars as likely
to be in large part genuine works of Ephraem.[55]
Their authenticity is perceived in their general con-
gruity with ideas found expressed in the genuine
hymns and homilies.[56]

As in the case of the hymns and homilies, so in
regard to the more straightforward biblical commentaries, it is clear that later texts have been attributed to Ephraem because of the popularity and
authority of his name. And just as in the instance of
the hymns and homilies the new attributions were
made in a tradition of on-going liturgical requirements, so in the case of the commentaries it is not
unlikely that a certain school tradition was the
setting for the attribution of commentaries on the
books of the Old Testament *Peshitta* to Ephraem.
This likelihood is increased when one takes notice of
the polemical character of much of the exegesis, even
in the commentaries on Genesis and Exodus.[57] For
this is the most likely milieu for the transmission of

Ephraem's *Prose Refutations* as well, the texts in which the adversaries of record in the Syriac-speaking communities are refuted, principally Marcion, Bar Daiṣān, and Mani.[58]

Another dimension of Ephraem's Old Testament commentary which most modern scholars seldom fail to mention is the Jewish connection. It is not only the fact that the Syriac versions he and his continuators and imitators used have the Hebrew Bible rather than the Septuagint behind them, but that many aspects of the interpretation have their closest analogues in the Jewish exegetical tradition rather than in other Christian traditions.[59] This is a dimension of Ephraem's thought which is perceptible not only in the straightforward commentaries, but in the hymns and homilies as well.[60] It reminds the modern reader of Ephraem's work that in the Christian world of the Semitic languages there was a certain continuity of thought and imagination with the Jewish world about the interpretation of the biblical narratives that one does not always find in Greek and Latin commentaries.[61]

Ephraem is also credited with commentaries on most of the New Testament books. There are works on the Acts of the Apostles and the Pauline epistles, which survive only in Armenian translations,[62] and which have not been much studied, along with his well known and often quoted commentary on Tatian's *Diatessaron*. Although the text survives in only a single manuscript in the original Syriac,[63] and in two manucripts in Armenian translation,[64] Dom Louis Leloir pronounced it to be "the most important of Ephrem's exegetical works."[65] But in a series

of a half dozen articles, in which he subjects portions
of the commentary to an intense literary scrutiny,
based on comparisons with passages in the surely
genuine hymns and homilies, Dom Edmund Beck
came to the conclusion that "Ephraem was not the
author of the commentary. On the other hand, the
many and large connections with Ephraem's hymns
and homilies allow the supposition that the work
originates from his school."[66]

Once again one encounters the situation in
which Ephraem's work has been taken over into a
tradition which then augments and expands it, all
the while relying on the popularity and authority of
the deacon of Nisibis and Edessa to commend it to
successive generations of readers and users. As for
Ephraem's own attitude to the scriptures and their
interpretation, there is a passage in the commentary
on the *Diatessaron* which, even if it may not have
come from his pen, is nevertheless an apt expression
of his point of view. The text says,

> Many are the perspectives of his word, just as many
> are the perspectives of those who study it. [God] has
> fashioned his word with many beautiful forms, so that
> each one who studies it may consider what he likes. He has
> hidden in his word all kinds of treasures so that each one
> of us, wherever we meditate, may be enriched by it. His
> utterance is a tree of life, which offers you blessed fruit
> from every side. It is like that rock which burst forth in the
> desert, becoming spiritual drink to everyone from all
> places. [They ate] spiritual food and drank spiritual drink.
> (1 Cor. 10:3-4)
>
> Therefore, whoever encounters one of its riches must
> not think that that alone which he has found is all that is

in it, but [rather] that it is this alone that he is capable of
finding from the many things in it. Enriched by it, let him
not think that he has impoverished it. But rather let him
give thanks for its greatness, he that is unequal to it.
Rejoice that you have been satiated, and do not be upset
that it is richer than you.... Give thanks for what you have
taken away, and do not murmur over what remains and is
in excess. That which you have taken and gone away with
is your portion and that which is left over is also your
heritage.[67]

V

Ephraem shares with his audience the sense of
awe with which he is filled as he approaches the book
of Genesis in the composition of his *Hymns on
Paradise.* In several stanzas he provides a concise
statement of his customary posture in regard to the
Bible. He says,

In his book Moses
        described the creation of the natural world,
so that both Nature and Scripture
        might bear witness to the Creator:
Nature, through man's use of it,
        Scripture, through his reading of it.
These are the witnesses
        which reach everywhere,
they are to be found at all times,
        present at every hour,
confuting the unbeliever
        who defames the Creator.

I read the opening of this book
        and was filled with joy,

for its verses and lines
    spread out their arms to welcome me;
the first rushed out and kissed me,
    and led me on to its companion;
and when I reached that verse
    wherein is written
the story of Paradise,
    it lifted me up and transported me
from the bosom of the book
    to the very bosom of Paradise.

The eye and the mind
    traveled over the lines
as over a bridge, and entered together
    the story of Paradise.
The eye as it read
    transported the mind;
in return the mind, too,
    gave the eye rest
from its reading,
    for when the book had been read
the eye had rest
    but the mind was engaged.

Both the bridge and the gate
    of Paradise
did I find in this book.
    I crossed over and entered;
my eye remained outside
    but my mind entered within.
I began to wander
    amid things not described.
This is a luminous height,
    clear, lofty and fair:
Scripture named it Eden,
    the summit of all blessings.[68]

These few stanzas elegantly portray Ephraem in the posture of what in the west we would call *lectio divina*, and they include the mention of ideas which he took for granted whenever he opened his Bible.[69] If we are to read the scriptures along with him we must examine these ideas in some more detail. They are basically three: both Nature and Scripture bear witness to the Creator; the verses of scripture provide a bridge to Paradise; beyond the written or proclaimed words of the Bible, the attentive mind gains access to the luminous heights, the summit of all blessings.

A - Nature and Scripture

Ephraem voices the idea that Nature and Scripture are the twin sources of revelation at several places in his writings. In a *madrāshâ* in which he had been reviewing some ways in which Nature reveals its Creator he says,

Look and see how Nature and Scripture
      are yoked together for the Husbandman:
Nature abhors adulterers,
      practicers of magic and murderers;
      Scripture abhors them too.
Once Nature and Scripture had cleaned the land
      – they sowed in it new commandments
      in the land of the heart, so that it might bear fruit,
      praise for the Lord of Nature
      glory for the Lord of Scripture.[70]

In another passage Ephraem likens Nature and the two testaments of Scripture to three lyres, to the

accompaniment of which the Word of God sings;
the lyre of Nature then testifies that it is the Saviour
himself who sings to the lyre of Moses and the lyre
of the Gospel. Ephraem says,

> The Word of the Most High came down
>   and clothed himself in
> a weak body with two hands.[71]
> He took up and balanced two lyres,
> one in his right hand and one in his left.
> A third he put in front of him,
> to be a witness for the other two;
> for it was the middle lyre corroborating
> that their Lord was singing to their accompaniment.[72]

For Ephraem the Bible is the rule of faith which
even Nature confirms. As he says, "Faith in the
scriptures is the second soul."[73] And he means the
integral scriptures, the Old and New Testaments
together—the Christian Bible, which has Christ as
its focal point. He says,

> In the Torah Moses trod
> the Way of the 'mystic symbols'[74] before that People
> who used to wander every which way.
> But our Lord, in his testaments,
> definitively established the path of Truth
> for the Peoples who came to the Way of Life.[75]
> All the 'mystic symbols' thus travelled
> on that Way which Moses trod
> and were brought to fulfillment in the Way of the Son.
> Let our mind then become
> cleared land for that Way.
> Instead of on the ground, my brothers,
> let us, on souls, tread the Way of Life.[76]

For Ephraem, only the integral scriptures can be
the measure of truth. He says in the *Hymns against
Heresies*,

> Like the body of the alphabet,
> which is complete in its members,
> neither subtracting a letter,
> nor adding another one,
> so is the Truth which is written
> in the Holy Gospel,
> in the letters of the alphabet,
> he perfect measure which does not accept
> less or more.[77]

According to Ephraem, in the Bible's verses,
with their types and images, and their fulfillment in
Christ, he finds that Christ himself is the bridge and
the gate to Paradise. That is because the prophets
and the apostles, that is to say the Bible, are the
milestones and the inns respectively,[78] on the Way of
Life, and they all lead to Christ who alone reveals his
Father. According to Ephraem, as Sebastian Brock
has put it, "what is 'hidden' in the symbols of Nature
and of Scripture is revealed in Christ at the Incarnation."[79]

B - The Bridge over the Chasm

For Ephraem, the Scriptures, and Christ himself, are a bridge which God's love provides over the
ontological chasm that separates created beings from
their Creator. He speaks of this chasm primarily in
the *Hymns on Faith*, where his adversaries are the
Arians, or perhaps more precisely the 'Homoeans.'[80]

He says,

> Let us not allow ourselves to go astray
>> and to study our God.
> Let us take the measure of our mind,
>> and gauge our thinking.
> And as for our knowledge, let us know how small it is, and
> too contemptible to scrutinize the Knower of all.

> Tell me, how will you have pictured in your mind that
> birth,[81] so far removed from the range of your inquiry?
> Do you think there is just a short gap in the interval
> between you and searching it out?

> Seal your mouth with silence; let your tongue not act rashly.
> Know yourself, a creature made, son of one so fashioned,
> that there is a great chasm (*peḥtâ*) without bottom
> between you and the Son, at the edge of scrutiny.[82]

In another passage from the same collection of *madrāshê* Ephraem makes the point more simply. He says,

> As for 'Deity,'
>> what man (*ʿabdâ*)
> can search it out?
>> There is a chasm (*peḥtâ*) between him
> and the Creator.

> As for 'Deity,'
>> it is not far removed
> from its chattels (*qenyānê*);
>> there is love between it
> and the creatures.[83]

These passages are sufficient to record Ephraem's sense of the chasm between the creature and the Creator. One notices that it is explicitly a chasm in knowledge and not in love.[84] Thomas Koonammakkal sums up Ephrem's thought in these words:

> The far-awayness and great closeness of God, is a much repeated theme in Ephrem... . Nature and Scripture are two treasuries of the self-revealing God who put on human language for our sake. These treasuries are full of types, symbols and metaphors. But the key to open these and interpret the mysteries, is the Incarnate Son.[85]

It is in this sense that for Ephraem the lines of the scriptures form a bridge over the ontological chasm, bringing the human mind not only into Paradise, but, by way of the incarnate Son of God, to the Godhead itself. For just as in the Son, God clothed himself in flesh, in the scriptures, one might say, God clothed himself in human words. Ephraem put it this way:

> Let us give thanks to God who clothed Himself in the
>   names of the body's various parts:
> Scripture refers to His 'ears,' to teach us that He listens
>   to us;
> it speaks of His 'eyes,' to show that He sees us.
> It was just the names of such things that He put on,
> and, although in His true Being there is not wrath or
>   regret,
> yet He put on these names too because of our weakness.
>
> We should realize that, had He not put on the names
> of such things, it would not have been possible for Him

to speak with us humans. By means of what belongs
    to us did He draw close to us:
He clothed Himself in our language, so that He might
    clothe us
in His mode of life.[86]

The incarnate Word of God is then himself the
ultimate bridge to the Father. Ephraem makes this
point clearly in a prayer he addresses to Jesus as the
final strophe in an acrostic *madrāshê* which ends
with the middle letter of the Syriac alphabet, *yodh*,
the first letter of the name 'Jesus' (*Yeshûʿ*). He says,

> O Jesus, glorious name,
> hidden bridge which carries one over
> from death to life,
> I have come to a stop with you;
> I finish with your letter *yodh*.
> Be a bridge for my words
> to cross over to your truth.
> Make your love a bridge for your servant.
> By means of you I shall cross over to your Father.
> I will cross over and say, 'Blessed is the One
> who has made his might tender in his offspring.'[87]

C - The Mind Enters Within

According to Ephraem, when one reads the
scriptures the eye remains outside, but the mind
enters within and wanders among things indescrib-
able. That is because it is by means of the mind
(*tarʿîtâ*) that one encounters the majesty of God. In
the *Prose Refutations* Ephraem says,

Moses testifies that while it was granted to him to do everything like God, at last he abandoned everything and prayed to see the Lord of all. For if the creatures of the Creator are so pleasant to look upon, how much more pleasant is their Creator to look upon; but because we have not any eye which is able to look upon his splendour, a mind (*tar'îtâ*) was given us which is able to contemplate his beauty.[88]

In one of the *Hymns on Paradise* Ephraem further specifies his view of the mind's role in the human encounter with God. He says,

Far more glorious than the body
    is the soul,
and more glorious still than the soul
    is the mind,
but more hidden than the mind
    is the Godhead.
At the end
    the body will put on
the beauty of the soul,
    the soul will put on that of the mind,
while the mind shall put on
    the very likeness of God's majesty.[89]

The mind puts on the very likeness of God's majesty because in Nature and in Scripture the eye's perusal brings to the mind's eye the types and images, indeed the very reality of God incarnate, to whom all images and types point, in seeing whom one sees the Father. As Ephraem says in another *madrāshâ*, speaking of God the Father in relation to the Son incarnate:

Glory be to that Powerful One
    who painted for himself
a portrait for his majesty
    and an image for his invisibility.
In the eye and in the mind,
    in both of them, we have seen Him.[90]

Here is not the place to enter into a discussion of Ephraem's psychology and theory of knowledge.[91] Suffice it now to say only that for him the mind (*tarᶜîtâ* or *reᶜyānâ*) can be likened to a mirror (*maḥzîtâ*) in which one sees the types and symbols from Nature and Scripture, which themselves in turn function like a mirror in which one sees the hidden things of God. Therefore, Ephraem says, the scriptures too are like a mirror which God has set up for the mind's eye, in which one might see the triune God.[92] He says,

The scriptures are set up
    like a mirror;
one whose eye is clear
    sees there
the image of the truth.

Set up there
    is the image of the Father;
depicted there
    is the image of the Son,
and of the Holy Spirit.[93]

VI

According to Ephraem, what one finds in Nature and Scripture are the types and symbols, along with the names and titles, in terms of which the invisible God reveals himself to the eyes and minds of persons of good faith, and which prepare them to recognize the incarnate Word of God in Jesus of Nazareth. In one stanza from his *Hymns on Virginity* Ephraem says the following about the incarnate Son and his symbols and types:

> In every place, if you look, his symbol is there,
> and wherever you read, you will find his types.
> For in him all creatures were created
> and he traced his symbols on his property.
> When he was creating the world,
> he looked to adorn it with icons of himself.
> The springs of his symbols were opened up to run down and
> pour forth his symbols into his members.[94]

In another *madrāshâ* Ephraem speaks similarly of the symbols and types of God's Son and Messiah to be found in the scriptures. He says, in allusion to the Arianism which he combats:

> Those doctrines are put to shame
>   which have alienated the Son.
> See, the Law carries
>   all the likenesses of him.
> See, the Prophets, like deacons,
>   carry
> the icons of the Messiah.
> Nature and the scriptures
>   together carry
> the symbols of his humanity
>   and of his divinity.[95]

It is in the scriptures too that God teaches human beings the names and titles which reveal what they can know of God himself. Ephraem says,

> His names will instruct you,
>> how and what you should call him.
> One teaches you he is the 'Eternal One,'
>> another that he is the 'Creator.'
> One shows you he is the 'Good One,'
>> another informs you he is the 'Just One.'
> He is also named and called
>> 'Father.'
> The scriptures are the crucible;
>> why does the fool gainsay it?
> Contemplate in his crucibles,
>> his names and his distinctions.
> For he has names,
>> perfect and exact;
> he also has names
>> metaphorical and transient... .
> Have a care for his names,
>> perfect and holy,
> for if you deny one
>> they will all fly away.
> They are tied to one another
>> and they carry all,
> like the pillars
>> of the world.[96]

These symbols and types, names and titles, which for Ephraem are the very contents of the scriptures, are also the idiom of his own religious discourse. They are the basic elements of the narratives of the patriarchs and prophets read through the lens of the Gospel and the person of the incarnate Word, the names of God and of his creatures revealed and interpreted according to their obvious senses in the text. In turn they become the paradigms for the Christian's own understanding of God and the world, the terms of one's theology of the Trinity and the Incarnation, of Christology, sacramentology, ecclesiology, anthropology and eschatology.[97] Ephraem read the scriptures in terms of these symbols, types, names and titles, and they in turn became the terms of his own thought. For this reason some scholars have used the expression "symbolic theology" to characterize Ephraem's approach to religious discourse, and they often contrast it to Greek or Latin modes of thought, not to mention modern systematic theology.[98] Consequently, the better to understand Ephraem's reading of the Bible, one must for a moment look more closely at how he thinks about the symbols and types, the names and titles,[99] which he himself so deftly employs in his own writings.

First of all, it is important to make the point that while one will surely find many examples of 'typological' exegesis in Ephraem's works, of the sort that scholars regularly associate with the so-called 'Antiochene' school of biblical interpretation and its exercise of *theoria*,[100] the role of symbols, types, names and titles in his thought goes well beyond this limited range of applicability. For him they are the very idiom of human thought in general, and of what we call 'theology' in particular. One may say that for Ephraem, on both the natural and the supernatural planes, "that which one knows is a series of images and words which are stored in the mind. One does not possess the reality itself."[101]

In the divine revelation, what one most often finds, according to Ephraem, even in the names and titles of God, are manifest symbols, which he most often calls *râzê* (sing. *râzâ*) in Syriac, which in turn, by God's grace, disclose to the human mind those aspects of the hidden reality or truth (*shrārâ, qushtâ*) which are within the range of the capacities of human intelligence. To pry further than this into the essence of God, is to fall into the chasm that separates the creature from the Creator, and to wander in error. Religious thought or 'theology' then rightfully consists in the contemplation of the *râzê*, the mystic symbols in which God reveals the truth about himself and the world to human beings.

The term *râzâ* came to Syriac via ancient Persian and old Aramaic, where it basically meant 'secret', and in this sense it appears in the book of Daniel (e.g., Dan. 2:18). Ephraem and other Syriac writers use the word more in the sense of a 'mystic symbol', which is not so much mysterious in its function as it is indicative, disclosing to human minds according to their capacities what is hidden from human knowledge in its essence, such as the being of God and the course of the economy of salvation. While *râzâ* is often synomous with 'type' (*typos, ṭupsâ*) in Ephraem's works, his use of the term goes well beyond what one normally thinks of as the typological sense of the scriptures, i.e., words, actions, facts, and narratives in the Old Testament that foreshadow their models in the New Testament. For Ephraem, biblical typologies are indeed *râzê*, but so are many things in nature, and also in the apostolic kerygma and the life of the church, like sacraments.

For him, the *râzê* all point to the incarnate Christ, who is "the Lord of the *râzê*, who fulfills all *râzê* in his crucifixion."[102] So they may point forward from Nature and Scripture to Christ, who in turn reveals his Father to the eye of faith, or they point from the church's life and liturgy back to Christ, who in turn reveals to the faithful believer the events of the eschaton, the ultimate fulfillment of all creation in the economy of salvation.[103]

The image of the image maker is one of Ephraem's favorite figures of speech,[104] and he uses it to advantage in two stanzas of the *Hymns on Virginity* to give a good summary of the functioning of the *râzê* in his thought. In these stanzas, Ephraem addresses himself to Christ, "the painter of his own *râzê*,"[105] as he calls him in another place. He says,

> Scattered *râzê* you have gathered up
>   from the Torah for your comeliness.
> You have published the models (*tapeṇkê*)
>   which are in your Gospel,
>   along with the prodigies and signs of nature.
> You have mixed them together as the paints for
>   your portrait; you have looked at yourself,
>   and painted your own portrait.
> Here is the painter, who in himself has painted
>   his Father's portrait;
>   two portrayed, the one in the other.
> The prophets, the kings, and the priests,
>   who were creatures, all of them painted
>   your portrait, but they themselves bore no resemblance.
> Created beings are not capable;
>   you alone are capable of painting the portrait.
> They indeed drew the lines of your portrait;

you in your coming brought it to completion.
The lines then disappeared due to the strength of the paints,
the most brilliant of all colors.[106]

VII

Given the ever suggestive intricacy of his rich
imagination, it seems somehow rash to lay down
laws for Ephraem's biblical exegesis.[107] He himself
insists on the multiple possibilities of every scripture
passage. At one point in the *Commentary on the
Diatessaron* he says,

If there were [only] one meaning for the words [of
Scripture], the first interpreter would find it, and all other
listeners would have neither the toil of seeking nor the
pleasure of finding. But every word of our Lord has its own
image, and each image has many members, and each
member possesses its own species and form. Each person
hears in accordance with his capacity, and it is interpreted
in accordance with what has been given to him.[108]

We find Ephraem's own exegesis basically in
two forms; somewhat sparingly in the straightforward commentaries on several biblical books: Genesis, Exodus, and the text of the *Diatessaron*; and
much more abundantly in the numerous *mêmrê* and
madrāshê on particular theological or liturgical
themes. Nowhere does he discuss principles of exegesis as such; everywhere his methods are clear and
evident; he begins with the literal meaning of the
text, and then he looks for the spiritual sense en-
coded in the symbols and types, the names and titles
which have the incarnate son of God as their con-

stant point of reference. In this way the integral, Christian Bible is the constant measure of his thought, supplying the very idiom of his religious discourse.

In his commentaries on Genesis and Exodus Ephraem does not discuss each verse. Rather, he concentrates on the passages of greatest importance, such as the creation narratives, where there is much at issue for his polemics against adversaries like the Marcionites, the followers of Bar Daiṣan and Mani. He seems to be in a hurry, as if the commentaries are meant to serve only some immediate, academic purpose. At the end of his discussion of passages in Genesis, for example, when he comes to the account of Jacob's blessings for his sons (Gen. 49: 2-27), and after he has set out what according to him the text literally means, he says:

> Now that we have spoken of the literal meaning (*suʿrānaʾit*) of the blessings of Jacob, let us go back and speak of their spiritual meaning (*rûḥānaʾit*) as well. We did not fittingly speak of their literal meaning nor will we write of their spiritual meaning as we ought, for we spoke too sparingly of their literal meaning and we will write of their spiritual meaning much too briefly.[109]

Not only is Ephraem's feeling of haste evident in this paragraph, but what he says allows one to see that he expressly recognizes two senses of the scriptural text, the literal sense and the spiritual sense. In the sequel it is evident that for him the spiritual sense consists in whatever there is in the terms of the blessings that one might take to refer to the ultimate economy of salvation in Christ and in the church, the types and symbols of what is yet to come in the unfolding of the history of salvation. In other passages he indicates the spiritual sense almost *en passant*. For example, in his comment on Gen. 22:13, a verse at the end of the account of Abraham's sacrifice of Isaac in which his version of the text reads, "Then Abraham saw a ram in a tree, took it, and offered it upon the altar in the place of his son," Ephraem says,

> The mountain spit out the tree and the tree the ram, so that in the ram that hung in the tree and had become the sacrifice in the place of Abraham's son, there might be depicted the day of Him who was to hang upon the wood like a ram and was to taste death for the sake of the whole world.[110]

The commentary on the *Diatessaron* is a more leisurely work for Ephraem. Although he does not cover the whole text, he takes his time in commenting not only on the literal meaning of the words in the verses he discusses, but he also frequently enlarges on a theme which the text suggests, often in the process recalling the types and symbols from Old Testament narratives which find their point of reference in the Gospel. For example, in his reflections on the account of the crucifixion of Christ he does not fail to recall the story of Abraham's sacrifice of Isaac and the significance of the ram caught in the branches of the tree.[111] In fact, the *leitmotiv* of his commentary is the idea that the church, which was previously hidden in mysteries, is now openly proclaiming God's true revelation. At the beginning of the *Commentary* he says,

Although the Church was hidden, the mysteries were proclaiming it, while it remained itself silent. But then, when the Church itself became manifest, it began to interpret the mysteries, its erstwhile interpreters, which are silent [from now on] because of this revelation [of the church].[112]

The 'mysteries' of which he speaks are the *râzê* of the Old Testament now fully revealed in the New Testament and in the life of the church. If Ephraem stopped here, one could say, as many have, that his exegesis is an exercise in Antiochene *theoria* and leave it at that. But in his *mêmrê* and *madrāshê*, as we have seen, the *râzê* from Nature and Scripture, incorporating the symbols and types, the names and titles which God has revealed, carry the human mind by way of faith into the very depths of the mystery that is the Incarnation of the Son of God. So for Ephraem reading the Bible is really a *lectio divina* that carries the contemplative eye of the mind well beyond the limits of knowledge and leads it to the brink of faith and prayer. He says himself, in the *Homilies on Faith*:

If you just say God's name,
　　　there is no investigation underway.
Between God and man,
　　　faith is what is required.
If you put faith in Him, you honor Him;
　　　if you investigate Him, you belittle Him.
Between man and God then,
　　　there is to be but faith and prayer.[113]

In two stanzas of a hymn in the collection of his *Hymns on Faith* Ephraem makes clear his ideas about the role of this virtue in the mystical union of a human being with God. It is by means of faith that one is configured into the image of the Godhead, which is of course, in Ephraem's thought, the incarnate son of God. Ephraem says,

> The body then,
>   this mortal one,
> depends on the soul,
>   and the soul depends
> on faith.
>   But faith in turn
> depends on
>   the Godhead,
> since from the Father
>   there proceeds, in his Son,
> the Truth which enlivens
>   all in the Spirit.
>
> Then, in this reality [of faith],
>   mankind can
> bind himself
>   to the heavenly ones.
> In the soul he lives,
>   and by means of the body,
> he sees and hears.
>   In faith,
> love and wisdom,
>   he is united (*metmazag*) with
> the Godhead,
>   and is configured into its image.[114]

The person of faith is united with the Godhead in being configured into the image of the Godhead, the incarnate Son, God's only one (*îhîdāyâ*), in whom he has been invested at Baptism.[115] Him he recognizes in the mysteries (*râzê*) of Nature, Scripture and Church which all enter into his mind through eye and ear, there by name and title to depict the incarnate Son in whom he meets the Father, and through whom he receives the Spirit.

The Bible for Ephraem is then primarily a treasury of the symbols and types, the names and titles, which the incarnate Son has put on concretely for the purpose of leading all human beings to himself. It is for this reason that one says that in reading the Bible with St. Ephraem the Syrian, one engages not so much in theology, in the Augustinian sense of *fides quarens intellectum*, but in a contemplative *lectio divina* which is more like *fides adorans mysterium*. Its idiom is not primarily expository prose but a poetry akin to that of the Psalms which is more likely than not to induce silence in response to the awesome wonder.

Notes

* I owe this phrase to Robert Murray, S.J., *Symbols in Church and Kingdom; a Study in Early Syriac Tradition* (Cambridge: Cambridge University Press, 1975), p. 89, where he characterizes Ephraem's theology as, "Not *fides quaerens intellectum* but *fides adorans mysterium!*"

1 See C. Butler, *The Lausiac History of Palladius* (2 vols., Texts and Studies, 6; Cambridge, 1898 & 1904), vol. II, pp. 126-27.

[2] J. Bidez & G.H. Hansen (eds.), *Sozomenus, Kirchengeschichte* (GCS, 50; Berlin, 1960), pp. 127-30.

[3] See E.C. Richardson (ed.), *Hieronymus,* Liber de Viris Inlustribus (TU, 14; Leipzig, 1896), p. 51.

[4] In Sermon 42, Theodore proposed to his monks the ascetical example of John Chrysostom and of "Ephraem, famous in song." See S. Theodori Studitae Parva Catechesis in A. Mai, *Nova Patrum Bibliotheca* (vol. IX; Rome, 1888), p. 102.

[5] See M. Geerard, *Clavis Patrum Graecorum* (vol. II; Turnhout: Brepols, 1974), pp. 366-468.

[6] In spite of the large number of manuscripts purporting to contain works by Ephraem in Greek (one informed estimate speaks of two or three thousand of them), very few scholars have ever concerned themselves with their study. To date only three editions of collections of these texts have appeared, and these were published in the seventeenth and the eighteenth centuries. In 1616 in Cologne, G. Vossius published a comprehensive edition of the Greek Ephraem texts known to him under the title Opera Omnia. (See G. Vossius, *S. Ephraemi Syri Opera Omnia* (3 vols.; Cologne, 1616). In 1709 the Oxford scholar E. Thwaites brought out a folio edition of such works of Ephraem "translated into Greek," as he called them, which he could find among the manuscripts kept in the Bodleian library. (See E. Thwaites, Τὰ τοῦ ὁσίου πατρὸς Ἐφραιμ τοῦ Σύρου πρὸς τὴν Ἑλλάδα μεταβληθεντα (Oxford, 1709). Later in the century, in Rome, J.S. Assemani included Thwaites' edition, plus many other texts, in the first three volumes of his monumental edition of Ephraem's works. (See J.S. Assemani, *Sancti Patris Nostri Ephraem Syri Opera Omnia quae exstant Graece, Syriace, Latine* (vols. I-III; Rome, 1732, 1743, 1746). On these texts see the pioneering studies of Democratie Hemmerdinger-Iliadou, "L'authenticité sporadique de l'Éphrem grec," in *Akten des XI. internationalen Byzantinisten-Kongresses* (München, 1960), pp. 232-36; "Les doublets de l'édition de l'Éphrem grec par Assemani,"

Orientalia Christiana Periodica 24 (1958), pp. 371-382; "Vers une nouvelle édition de l'Éphrem grec," in *Studia Patristica* 3 (1961), pp. 72-80; "Éphrem Grec," & "Éphrem Latin," in *Dictionnaire de Spiritualité*, vol. IV (1960-1961), cols. 800-19; "Les citations évangéliques de l'Éphrem grec," *Byzantina* 4 (1973), pp. 315-73; "Éphrem: versions grecque, latine et slave: addenda et corrigenda," *Epeteris Hetaireias Byzantinon Spoudon* (1975-1976), pp. 320-59. See also J. Kirchmeyer & D. Hemmerdinger-Iliadou, "Saint Éphrem et le 'Liber Scintillarum'," *Recherches de Science Religieuse* 46 (1958), pp. 545-50. None of the Greek works attributed to Ephraem are now to be found in any manuscript witness prior to the tenth century. Nevertheless, there is the testimony of Photius, from around the years 855-56, to the effect that he was in his time aware of a collection of ascetical texts ascribed to Ephraem. See Jacques Schamp, "Éphrem de Nisibe et Photios: pour une chasse aux textes à travers la Bibliothèque," *Le Muséon* 98 (1985), pp. 293-314. From Greek many of the texts attributed to Ephraem were translated into most of the languages of Christian antiquity: Latin, Coptic, Arabic, and Old Slavonic, thereby ensuring his fame. There is a particularly rich "Ephraem" heritage in Latin translation. See, e.g., August C. Mahr, *Relations of Passion Plays to St. Ephrem the Syrian* (Colombus, Ohio: Wartburg Press, 1942; G. Bardy, "Le souvenir de saint Éphrem dans le haut-moyen âge latin," *Revue du Moyen Âge Latin* 2 (1946), pp. 297-300; Daniel Verhelst, "Scarpsum de Dictis Sancti Efrem prope Fine Mundi," in R. Lievens et al., (eds.), *Pascua Mediaevalia; Studies voor Prof. Dr. J. M. De Smet* (Leuven, 1983), pp. 518-28; T. S. Pattie, "Ephraem the Syrian and the Latin Manuscripts of 'De Paenitentia'," *The British Library Journal* 13 (1987), pp. 1-24; idem, "Ephraem's 'On Repentance' and the Translation of the Greek Text into Other Languages," *The British Library Journal* 16 (1990), pp. 174-85. The works of Ephraem Graecus were well known in the Arabic-speaking world of

the 'Melkites' who lived in the world of Islam. See W.
Heffening, "Die griechische Ephraem-Paraenesis gegen das
Lachen in arabischer Übersetzung," *Oriens Christianus* 3rd
series 2 (1927), pp. 94-119; J. M. Sauget, "Le dossier
éphrémien du manuscrit arabe Strasbourg 4226 et de ses
membra disiecta," *Orientalia Christiana Periodica* 42 (1978),
pp. 426-58; Samir Khalil, "L'Éphrem arabe, état des travaux,"
Symposium Syriacum 1976 (Orientalia Christiana Analecta,
205; Rome, 1978), pp. 229-40. In Kievan Rus,' the works
of Ephraem Graecus were especially dear to the influential
monk Abraham of Smolensk, whose principal disciple even
adopted the religious name 'Ephraem.' From these begin-
nings Ephraem's name and fame spread widely in Russia.
See G. P. Fedotov, *The Russian Religious Mind: Kievan
Christianity, the 10th to the 13th Centuries* (New York,
1960), pp. 158-75; G. Podskalsky, *Christentum und
theologische Literatur in der kiever Rus' (988-1237)* (Munich,
1982), pp. 50, 101-04, 140; I. Ogren, *The Paraeneses of
Ephraem the Syrian: History of the Slavonic Translation*
[Russian] (Uppsala, 1989).

[7] See Sidney H. Griffith, "Images of Ephraem: the Syrian Holy
Man and his Church," *Traditio* (1989-1990), pp. 7-33;
Edward G. Mathews, Jr., "The Vita Tradition of Ephrem
the Syrian, the Deacon of Edessa," *Diakonia* 22 (1988-
1989), pp. 15-42.

[8] See Joseph P. Amar, "Byzantine Ascetic Monachism and
Greek Bias in the Vita Tradition of Ephrem the Syrian,"
Orientalia Christiana Periodica 58 (1992), pp. 123-56.

[9] On the significance of this title see Sidney H. Griffith,
"Asceticism in the Church of Syria: the Hermeneutics of
Early Syrian Monasticism," in Vincent L. Wimbush &
Richard Valantasis (eds.), *Asceticism* (New York: Oxford
University Press, 1995), pp. 220-45.

[10] See J. S. Assemani, *Sancti Patris Nostri Ephraem Syri Opera
Omnia quae exstant Graece, Syriace, Latine* (vols. IV-VI;
Rome, 1737, 1740, 1743). J.S. Assemani came to Rome

from Lebanon to study in the Maronite college in 1703. After ordination he secured a post in the Vatican Library. In 1715, and again in 1735, he returned to the Middle East to hunt and purchase manuscripts for the library. Subsequently he was consecrated Archbishop of Tyre and named the Prefect of the Vatican Library. On the work of J. S. Assemani, Étienne Awad Assemani, and Pierre Mobarak see Pierre Raphael, *Le rôle du Collège Maronite Romain dans l'orientalisme aux XVIIe et XVIIIe siècles* (Beyrouth: Université Saint Joseph, 1950), pp. 123-36, 137-39, 145-48.

[11] See the details presented in Joseph Melki, "S. Ephrem le Syrien, un bilan de l'édition critique," *Parole de l'Orient* 11 (1983), pp. 3-88; S. P. Brock, "A Brief Guide to the Main Editions and Translations of the Works of St. Ephrem," *The Harp* 3 (1990), pp. 7-29.

[12] See Benedict XV, "Principi apostolorum Petro," *Acta Apostolicae Sedis* 12 (1920), pp. 457-73.

[13] Beck published his last edition in 1979 (CSCO, vols. 412 & 413). In the end, in addition to numerous other studies, he produced 19 volumes of editions and translations of Syriac works attributed to Ephraem.

[14] The surest way bibliographically to control what is being published in Ephraem studies is to consult the on-going classified bibliography in Syriac studies compiled by Sebastian P. Brock in *Parole de l'Orient*: 1960-1970 - 4 (1973), pp. 393-465; 1971-1980 - 10 (1981-1982), pp. 291-412; 1981-1985 - 14 (1987), pp. 289-360; 1986-1990 - 17 (1992), pp. 211-301.

[15] A notable case in point is R. P. C. Hanson, *The Search for the Christian Doctrine of God* (Edinburgh: T & T Clark, 1988).

[16] See Koonammakkal Thoma Kathanar, "Changing Views on Ephrem," *Christian Orient* 14 (1993), pp. 113-30. See also the remarks of Sebastian Brock, "The Poetic Artistry of St Ephrem: an Analysis of H. Azym. III," *Parole de l'Orient* 6&7 (1975-1976), pp. 21-28.

[17] F. Crawford Burkitt, *Early Eastern Christianity; St. Margaret's Lectures on the Syriac-Speaking Church* (London: John Murray, 1904), pp. 95 & 99.

[18] J. B. Segal, *Edessa, 'the Blessed City'* (Oxford: Oxford University Press, 1970), p. 89.

[19] R. Murray, "Ephrem Syrus," *Catholic Dictionary of Theology* (vol. II; London, 1967), pp. 220-23. Murray reaffirmed his opinion in *Symbols of Church and Kingdom*, p. 31.

[20] John Tavener, "Thunder Entered Her," Virgin Classics, VC 5 45035 2, 1994. Ephraem's compositions, entitled "Thunder Entered Her," and "Hymns of Paradise," both in translations by Sebastian P. Brock, are pieces no. 4 & no. 5 on the CD.

[21] P. Bedjan, *Acta Martyrum et Sanctorum Syriace* (vol. III; Paris & Leipzig, 1892), p. 667. See now Joseph P. Amar, "A Metrical Homily on Holy Mar Ephrem by Mar Jacob of Sarug; Critical Edition of the Syriac Text, Translation and Introduction," *Patrologia Orientalis* (tome, 47, fasc. 1, no. 209; Turnhout: Brepols, 1995), pp. 32-33.

[22] See Addai Scher, "Mar Barḥadbšabba ᶜArbaya: Cause de la fondation des écoles," *Patrologia Orientalis* 4 (1908), p. 377. On the sense of the title *mpashshqānâ* as Barhadbshabbâ would have understood it, see A. Vööbus, *The Statutes of the School of Nisibis* (Stockholm, 1961), p. 73.

[23] Scher, "Mar Barhadbšabba," p. 382. Following the hagiographical tradition, E. R. Hayes claimed that Ephraem became a 'professor' in the school of Edessa shortly after his move there, and that he composed most of his writings in this position. See E. R. Hayes, *L'école d'Édesse* (Thèse pour le Doctorat d'Université, Université de Paris; Paris: Les Presses Modernes, 1930), p. 128.

[24] See Ephraem's own reflections of these events in his Julian hymns in E. Beck, *Des heiligen Ephraem des Syrers Hymnen de Paradiso und Contra Julianum* (CSCO, vols. 174 & 175; Louvain: Peeters, 1957). See also Sidney H. Griffith, "Ephraem the Syrian's Hymns 'Against Julian': Meditations

on History and Imperial Power," *Vigiliae Christianae* 41 (1987), pp. 238-66.

[25] See Ephraem's praises of the bishops he served in the hymns he composed in their honor in E. Beck, *Des heiligen Ephraem des Syrers Carmina Nisibena, erster Teil* (CSCO, vols. 218 & 219; Louvain: Peeters, 1961).

[26] See I. Guidi, *Chronica Minora* (CSCO, vol. 1; Paris, 1903), p.5.

[27] See Sidney H. Griffith, "Ephraem, the Deacon of Edessa, and the Church of the Empire," in Thomas Halton & Joseph P. Williman (eds.), *Diakonia: Studies in Honor of Robert T. Meyer* (Washington, D.C.: Catholic University of America Press, 1986), pp. 22-52; *idem,* "Ephraem the Syrian's Hymns 'Against Julian';" *idem,* " 'Faith Seeking Understanding' in the Thought of St. Ephraem the Syrian," in George C. Berthold (ed.), *Faith Seeking Understanding: Learning and the Catholic Tradition. Selected Papers from the Symposium and Convocation Celebrating the Saint Anselm College Centennial* (Manchester, N.H.: Saint Anselm College Press, 1991), pp. 35-55; *idem,* "Setting Right the Church of Syria: Saint Ephraem's Hymns against Heresies," to appear in a forthcoming Festschrift for Robert A. Markus.

[28] Edmund Beck, *Des heiligen Ephraem des Syrers Hymnen contra Haereses* (CSCO, vols. 169-70; Louvain: Peeters, 1957), LVI:10.

[29] See Beck, *Carmina Nisibena, erster Teil,* XVII:3.

[30] See Sidney H. Griffith, "Julian Saba, 'Father of the Monks' of Syria," *Journal of Early Christian Studies* 2 (1994), pp. 185-216, esp. p. 207.

[31] See Griffith, "Images of Ephraem," pp. 20-26. See also Griffith, "Asceticism in the Church of Syria."

[32] Amar, "A Metrical Homily on Holy Mar Ephrem," pp. 30-31.

[33] For English translations of these works see Edward G. Mathews, Jr. & Joseph P. Amar, *St. Ephrem the Syrian: Selected Prose Works; Commenary on Genesis, Commentary on*

Exodus, Homily on our Lord, Letter to Publius (Kathleen
McVey, ed., The Fathers of the Church, vol. 91; Washing-
ton, D.C.: The Catholic University of America Press, 1994);
Carmel McCarthy, *Saint Ephrem's Commentary on Tatian's
Diatessaron; an English Translation of* Chester Beatty *Syriac
MS 709 with Introduction and Notes* (Journal of Semitic
Studies Supplement, 2; Oxford: Osford University Press on
Behalf of the University of Manchester, 1993).

[34] See C. W. Mitchell, *S. Ephraim's Prose Refutations of Mani,
Marcion, and Bardaisan* (2 vols.; London & Oxford: Will-
iams and Norgate, 1912 & 1921).

[35] See the convenient presentation of the titles of Ephraem's
Syriac works listed by genre in Brock, "A Brief Guide to the
Main Editions and Translations," pp. 17-28.

[36] For a discussion of the *madrāshâ* as a literary form see Michael
Lattke, "Sind Ephraems Madrāšē Hymnen?" *Oriens
Christianus* 73 (1989), p. 38-43. Lattke concludes that Beck
and others have improperly called the *madrāshê* 'hymns,'
given the traditional definition of the hymn properly so
called. He says, "Im Gegensatz zum Thesaurus Syriacus ist
der Madrāš(ā) nicht eine 'hymnorum species' (1956) sondern
der Hymnus ist eine Spezies der Madrāšē." (p. 43)

[37] See the suggestions of J. Gribomont, "La tradition liturgique
des hymnes pascales de s. Éphrem," *Parole de l'Orient* 4
(1973), pp. 191-246.

[38] "Ephrem, Edessenae ecclesiae diaconus, multa Syro sermone
conposuit, et ad tantam venit claritudinem, ut post lectionem
Scripturarum publice in quibusdam ecclesiis eius scripta
recitentur." E. C. Richardson, *Hieronymus,* Liber de Viris
Inlustribus (Leipzig, 1896) p. 51.

[39] See Andrew Palmer, " 'A Lyre without a Voice,' the Poetics
and the Politics of Ephrem the Syrian," *ARAM* 5 (1993), pp.
371-99.

[40] See J. Schirmann, "Hebrew Liturgical Poetry and Christian
Hymnology," *The Jewish Quarterly Review* n.s. 44 (1953-
1954), pp. 123-61.

[41] See J. Grosdidier de Matons, *Romanos le Mélode et les origines de la poésie religieuse à Byzance* (Paris: Beauchesne, 1977); William L. Petersen, "The Dependence of Romanos the Melodist upon the Syriac Ephrem; its Importance for the Origin of the Kontakion," *Vigiliae Christianae* 39 (1985), pp. 171-87; *idem, The Diatessaron and Ephrem Syrus as Sources of Romanos the Melodist* (CSCO, vol. 475; Louvain: Peeters, 1985); idem, "The Dependence of Romanos the Melodist upon the Syriac Ephraem," in E. A. Livingstone (ed.), *Studia Patristica* (vol. XVIII,4; Kalamazoo, Mich.: Cistercian Publications & Leuven: Peeters, 1990), pp. 274-81; S. P. Brock, "From Ephrem to Romanos," in E. A. Livingstone (ed.), *Studia Patristica* (vol. XX; Leuven: Peeters, 1989), pp. 139-51.

[42] In this connection, one thinks in particular of the reported 150 hymns of Bar Daiṣān (154-222) and his son, Harmonios. See H. J. W. Drijvers, *Bar Daiṣān of Edessa* (Studia Semitica Neerlandica, 6; Assen, 1966). See also Palmer, "'A Lyre without a Voice,'" pp. 391-93. Ephraem himself, in his Hymns against Heresies, refers to Bardaiṣān's 150 *maḍrashê*, numbered after the model of David's Psalms, and in LIII:3 he describes how a *madrāshâ* is composed. See E. Beck, *Des heiligen Ephraem des Syrers Hymnen contra Haereses* (CSCO, vols. 169 & 170; Louvain: Peeters, 1957), LIII:3. See E. Beck, "Ephräms des Syrers Hymnen," in H. Becker & R. Kaczynski (eds.), *Liturgie und Dichtung: Festschrift für W. Dürig* (vol. I; St. Ottilien, 1983), pp. 345-79. It is noteworthy too that the Syriac *Vita* of Ephraem expressly makes the claim that Ephraem wrote his hymns to counteract the influence of Bardaiṣān's compositions. See Joseph P. Amar, "The Syriac *Vita* Tradition of Ephrem the Syrian" (Ph. D. Dissertation, The Catholic University of America, Washington, D. C., 1988), chap. 31. Nor should one forget the Psalms of Mani in Ephraem's background. In his own Hymns against Heresies Ephraem refers to Mani's *madrāshê*. See Beck, *Hymnen contra Haereses,* I:16.

[43] See the remarks of G. A. M. Rouwhorst, *Les hymnes pascales d'Ephrem de Nisibe* (2 vols.; Leiden: E. J. Brill, 1989), vol. I, pp. 24-25.

[44] See, e.g., the discussion of the hymns on Julian Saba in Griffith, "Julian Saba, 'Father of the Monks of Syria,'" esp. pp. 198-203.

[45] See B. Outtier, "Contribution à l'étude de la préhistoire des collections d'hymnes d'Éphrem," *Parole de l'Orient* 6 & 7 (1975-1976), pp. 49-61.

[46] The best discussions of the authenticity of the hymns and verse homilies attributed to Ephraem are to be found in the introductions to the critical editions and translations of the texts published by Dom Edmund Beck, O.S.B. in the CSCO, for which see the convenient list in Brock, "A Brief Guide to the Main Editions," pp. 28-29.

[47] See André De Halleux, "La transmission des Hymnes d'Éphrem d'après le MS. Sinai Syr. 10, f. 165v-178r," in *Symposium Syriacum 1972* (Orientalia Christiana Analecta, 197; Rome, 1974), pp. 21-36; *idem*, "Une clé pour les hymnes d'Éphrem dans le MS. Sinai Syr. 10," *Le Muséon* 85 (1972), pp. 171-99.

[48] Amar, "A Metrical Homily on Holy Mar Ephrem," # 48, p. 37.

[49] Presumably a reference to 1 Corinthians 14:34.

[50] Ephraem himself voiced this thought in one of his Hymns on Paradise. In Hymn VI:8 he is speaking of the church, "the assembly of the saints," where each day "the medicine of life" is available, and there too he goes on to say:

> The serpent (*hewyâ*) is crippled and bound
>> by the curse,
> while Eve's (*hawwâ*) mouth is sealed
> with a silence that is beneficial (Gen. 3:14)
> – but it also serves once again
> as a harp to sing the praises of her Creator.

Edmund Beck, *Des heiligen Ephraem des Syrers Hymnen De Paradiso und Contra Julianum* (CSCO, vols. 174 & 175; Louvain: Peeters, 1957), VI:8. The English translation is from Sebastian Brock, *Saint Ephrem the Syrian; Hymns on Paradise* (Crestwood, N.Y.: St Vladimir's Seminary Press, 1990), p. 111.

[51] Amar, "A Metrical Homily on Holy Mar Ephrem," ## 40-44, pp. 34-35.

[52] In this connection one should recall that the Syriac word *madrāshâ* is cognate with the Hebrew word for the well known genre of biblical interpretation, midrash.

[53] R. M. Tonneau, *Sancti Ephraem Syri in Genesim et in Exodum commentarii* (CSCO, vols. 152 & 153; Louvain: Peeters, 1955), vol. 152, p. 3. The English translation is from Mathews & Amar, *St. Ephrem the Syrian; Selected Prose Works*, p. 67.

[54] See the early survey by T.-J. Lamy, "L'exégèse en orient au IVe siècle ou les commentaires de saint Ephrem," *Revue Biblique* 2 (1893), pp. 5-25, 161-81, 465-86.

[55] There are some dissenters. See Paul Féghali, "Influence des Targums sur la pensée exégétique d'Éphrem?" in H. J. W. Drijvers et al. (eds.), *IV Symposium Syriacum 1984* (Orientalia Christiana Analecta, 229; Rome, 1987), pp. 71-82; *idem*, "Notes sur l'exégèse de s. Ephrem; commentaire sur le deluge (Gen. 6, 1-9, 17)," *Parole de l'Orient* 8 (1977-78), pp. 67-70. See also David Bundy, "Ephrem's Exegesis of Isaiah," in E. A. Livingstone (ed.), *Studia Patristica* (vol. 18, 4; Kalamazoo, Mich.: Cistercian Publications & Leuven: Peeters, 1990), pp. 235-37, who includes the commentary among the dubia ascribed to Ephraem, but cites the impressive list of scholars who accept its authenticity, including Dom Edmund Beck (p. 236). Actually, Beck names only the commentary on Genesis in his list of Ephraem's authentic works. See Edmond Beck, "Éphrem le Syrien (saint)," *Dictionnaire de Spiritualité* (vol. IV; Paris: Beauchesne, 1959), col. 790.

[56] See, in particular, the work of T. Jansma, "Ephraems Beschreibung des ersten Tages der Schöpfung; Bemerkungen über den Character seines Kommentars zur Genesis," *Orientalia Christiana Periodica* 37 (1971), pp. 295-316; idem, "Beiträge zur Berichtigung einzelner Stellen in Ephraems Genesiskommentar," *Oriens Christianus* 56 (1972), pp. 59-79; *idem*, "Ephraem's Commentary on Exodus," *Journal of Semitic Studies* 17 (1972), pp. 203-12; idem, "Ephraem on Exodus II, 5: Reflexions on the Interplay of Human Freewill and Divine Providence," *Orientalia Christiana Periodica* 39 (1973), pp. 5-28; *idem*, "Ephraem on Genesis xlix 10; an Enquiry into the Syriac Text Forms as Presented in his Commentary on Genesis," *Parole de l'Orient* 4 (1973), pp. 247-56; *idem*, "Weitere Beiträge zur Berichtigung einzelner Stellen in Ephraems Kommentare zu Genesis und Exodus," *Oriens Christianus* 58 (1974), pp. 121-131. See also Sten Hidal, *Interpretatio Syriaca; die Kommentare des heiligen Ephräm des Syrers zu Genesis und Exodus mit besondere Berücksichtigung ihrer Auslegungsgeschichtlichen Stellung* (Lund: Gleerup, 1974); Tryggve Kronholm, *Motifs from Genesis 1 - 11 in the Genuine Hymns of Ephrem the Syrian; with particular reference to the influence of Jewish exegetical tradition* (Lund: CWK Gleerup, 1978). It is also noteworthy in this connection that Sebastian Brock has appended an English translation of Ephraem's commentary on Genesis 2 & 3 to his translation of the Hymns on Paradise. See Brock, *St. Ephrem the Syrian; Hymns on Paradise*, pp. 197-227. Scholars are now beginning to study Ephraem's exegesis of other OT books as found in his genuine writings. See, e.g., Emidio Vergani, "La Verita' nella Fornace: l'esegesi di Dn 3 nella chiesa siriaca antica," (Tesi di dottorato; Bologna: Universita' degli Studi di Bologna, 1994/95).

[57] See Mathews and Amar, *St. Ephrem the Syrian; Selected Prose Works*, pp. 60-62, 218-19.

[58] On Ephraem's ideas about the adversaries, see Griffith, "Setting Right the Church of Syria."

[59] See, e.g., Féghali, "Influence des Targums," and Sebastian P. Brock, "Jewish Traditions in Syriac Sources," *Journal of Jewish Studies* 30 (1979), pp. 212-32.

[60] See, e.g., Kronholm, *Motifs from Genesis 1-11* and N. Sed, "Les hymnes sur le paradis de saint Ephrem et les traditions juives," *Le Muséon* 81 (1968), pp. 455-501.

[61] The matter is actually more complex than this. Some modern researchers are finding a remarkable participation by writers like Ephraem (and Narsai) in traditions of interpretation that are also to be found in certain apocryphal works, which in turn may have Jewish or Christian roots, or a combination of both. One thinks in particular of the ongoing work of Gary A. Anderson on the Adam and Eve traditions. See G. Anderson & M.E. Stone, *A Synopsis of the Books of Adam and Eve* (Early Judaism and its Literature, 5; Atlanta: Scholars Press, 1994); Gary A. Anderson, "The Penitence Narrative in the Life of Adam and Eve," *Hebrew Union College Annual* 64 (1993), pp. 1-38. Look for Anderson's forthcoming studies on "The Exaltation of Adam and the Fall of Satan in Light of Psalm 8:5," "The Penitence of Adam in Early Judaism and Christianity," "Psalm 8 and the Creation of Humankind," "Garments of Skin, Garments of Glory," "The Fall of Satan in the Vita and Ephrem."

[62] See N. W. Akinian, *Des hl. Ephraem Erklärung der Apostelgeschichte* (Wien, 1921); the Mechitarist Fathers, *S. Ephrem Syri Commentarii in Epistolas D. Pauli nunc primum ex Armenio in Latinum sermonem a Patribus Mekhitaristis translati* (Venice, 1893).

[63] See Louis Leloir, *Saint Ephrem: Commentaire de l'évangile concordant; texte syriaque (MS Chester Beatty 709)* (Chester Beatty Monographs, 8; Dublin, 1963), idem, *Saint Ephrem: Commentaire de l'évangile concordant; texte syriaque (MS Chester Beatty 709), folios additionnels* (Leuven & Paris: Peeters, 1990). An English translation of the text is available

in Carmel McCarthy, *Saint Ephrem's Commentary on Tatian's Diatessaron; an English Translation of* Chester Beatty *MS 709 with Introduction and Notes* (Journal of Semitic Studies Supplement, 2; Oxford: Oxford University Press on Behalf of the University of Manchester, 1993). See also the French translation by Louis Leloir, *Éphrem de Nisibe: Commentaire de l'évangile concordant ou Diatessaron, traduit du Syriaque et de l'Arménien* (Sources Chrétiennes, no. 121; Paris: Les Éditions du Cerf, 1966).

[64] See Louis Leloir, *Saint Ephrem: Commentaire de l'évangile concordant (version arménienne)* (CSCO, vol. 137; Louvain: Peeters, 1953); idem, *Saint Ephrem: Commentaire de l'évangile concordant (traduction latine)* (CSCO, vol. 145; Louvain: Peeters, 1954).

[65] Louis Leloir, *Doctrines et méthodes de s. Éphrem d'après son commentaire de l'Évangile concordant* (CSCO, vol. 220; Louvain: Peeters, 1961), p. 40.

[66] Edmund Beck, "Ephräm und der Diatessaronkommentar im Abschnitt über die Wunder beim Tode Jesu am Kreuz," *Oriens Christianus* 77 (1993), p. 119. Five earlier studies which led Beck to the same conclusion are: E. Beck, "Der syrische Diatessaronkommentar zu Jo. 1, 1-5," *Oriens Christianus* 67 (1983), pp. 1-31; idem, "Der syrische Diatessaronkommentar zu der unvergebbaren Sünde wider den Heiligen Geist übersetzt und erklärt," *Oriens Christianus* 73 (1989), pp. 1-37; idem, "Der syrische Diatessaronkommentar zu der Perikope von der Samariterin am Brunnen," *Oriens Christianus* 74 (1990), pp. 1-24; idem, "Der syrische Diatessaronkommentar zu der Perikope von der Sünderin, Luc. 7, 36-50," *Oriens Christianus* 75 (1991), pp. 1-15; idem, "Der syrische Diatessaronkommentar zur Perikope vom reichen Jüngling," *Oriens Christianus* 76 (1992), pp. 1-45. See also William L. Petersen, "Some Remarks on the Integrity of Ephrem's Commentary on the Diatessaron," in E. A. Livingstone (ed.), *Studia Patristica* (vol. 20; Leuven: Peeters, 1989), pp. 197-202.

[67] McCarthy, *Saint Ephrem's Commentary on Tatian's Diatessaron*, pp. 49-50.

[68] Beck, *Hymnen de Paradiso*, V:2-5. The English translation is from Brock, *St. Ephrem the Syrian; Hymns on Paradise*, pp. 102-04.

[69] There have been studies of Ephraem's methods of exegesis. See, e.g., C. Bravo, *Notas Introductorias a la Noematica de San Efren* (Excerpta ex dissertatione ad Lauream in Facultate Theologica Pontificiae Universitatis Gregorianae; Rome, 1956; L. Leloir, *Doctrines et méthodes de s. Éphrem d'après son commentaire de l'évangile concordant* (CSCO, vol. 220; Louvain: Peeters, 1961); S. Hidal, *Interpretatio Syriaca; die Kommentare des heiligen Ephräm des Syrers zu Genesis un Exodus mit besonderer Berücksichtigung ihrer Auslegungs-geschichtlichen Stellung* (Coniectanea Biblica, OT series, 6; Lund, 1974); P. Yousif, "Exegetical Principles of St Ephraem of Nisibis," in E. A. Livingstone (ed.), *Studia Patristica* (vol. XVIII, 4; Kalamazoo, Mich.: Cistercian Publications & Leuven: Peeters, 1990), pp. 296-302. The approach adopted here takes an entirely different tack.

[70] Beck, *Hymnen contra Haereses*, XXVIII:11. The English translation is from Brock, *St. Ephrem the Syrian; Hymns on Paradise*, p. 191.

[71] On the important image of clothing language in Ephraem and other Syriac writers see Sebastian P. Brock, "Clothing Metaphors as a Means of Theological Expression in Syriac Tradition," in M. Schmidt (ed.), *Typus, Symbol, Allegorie bei den östlichen Vätern und ihren Parallelen im Mittelalter* (Eichstätter Beiträge, 4; Eichstatt, 1982), pp. 11-40.

[72] Edmund Beck, *Des heiligen Ephraem des Syrers Hymnen de Virginitate* (CSCO, vols. 223 & 224; Louvain: Peeters, 1962), XXIX:1. See Kathleen E. McVey, *Ephrem the Syrian; Hymns* (The Classics of Western Spirituality; New York: Paulist Press, 1989), p. 390.

[73] Beck, *Hymnen contra Haereses*, XLI:11.

[74] The Syriac term behind this expression is *râzê* (sing. *râzâ*), which will come up for discussion below. Suffice it now to say that it includes the senses of the Greek terms 'type' and 'mystery' in similar contexts, but extends well beyond their reach in Syriac discourse.

[75] On the People/Peoples, or Nation/Nations (*ʿammâ* / *ʿammê*) motif in early Syriac texts see Murray, *Symbols of Church and Kingdom*, pp. 41-68.

[76] Beck, *Hymnen contra Haereses*, XXV:3.

[77] Beck, *Hymnen contra Haereses*, XXII:1.

[78] See Edmund Beck, *Des heiligen Ephraem des Syrers Hymnen de Fide* (CSCO, vols. 154 & 155; Louvain: Peeters, 1955), LXV:1. See also Beck, *Hymnen contra Haereses*, XXV:1 & XXVII:3. Ephraem develops the image of the Way quite extensively at a number of places in his works. See Edmund Beck, "Das Bild vom Weg mit Meilensteinen und Herbergen bei Ephräm," *Oriens Christianus* 65 (1981), pp. 1-39.

[79] Sebastian Brock, *The Luminous Eye; the Spiritual World Vision of Saint Ephrem the Syrian* (Cistercian Studies Series, 124; Kalamazoo, Mich.: Cistercian Publications, 1992), pp. 28-29.

[80] Many years ago Edmund Beck identified the 'Arians', loosely so-called, as Ephraem's principal adversaries in the Hymns on Faith and the Homilies on Faith. See Edmund Beck, *Die Theologie des hl. Ephraem in seinen Hymnen über den Glauben* (Studia Anselmiana, fasc. XXI; Città del Vaticano: Libreria Vaticana, 1949); *idem, Ephraems Reden über den Glauben; ihr theologischer Lehrgehalt und ihr geschichtlicher Rahmen* (Studia Anselmiana, fasc. XXXIII; Rome: Herder, 1953). See also Peter Bruns, "Arius hellenizans? - Ephräm der Syrer und die neoarianischen Kontroversen seiner Zeit; ein Beitrag zur Rezeption des Nizänums im syrischen Sprachraum," *Zeitschrift für Kirchengeschichte* 101 (1990), pp. 21-57. For the suggestion that Ephraem's arguments seem often to be directed against those 'Arians' who are more properly called 'Homoeans' one is indebted to a paper read by Mark

Weedman of Marquette University at the annual meeting of the North American Patristic Society, Loyola University, Chicago, 30 May-1 June, 1996, entitled, "Ephrem's Opponents in the Hymns on the Faith." On the parallels between the thought of Ephraem and the Cappadocians see Paul S. Russell, *St. Ephraem the Syrian and St. Gregory the Theologian Confront the Arians* (Moran Eth ò, 5; Kottayam, Kerala: St. Ephrem Ecumenical Research Institute, 1994).

[81] The 'birth' referred to here is the generation of the Son from the Father, the subject at issue in the controversies in which Ephraem was embroiled.

[82] Beck, *Hymnen de Fide*, XV:3-5.

[83] Beck, *Hymnen de Fide*, LXIX:11-12.

[84] This aspect of Ephraem's thinking has been examined thoroughly by Thomas Koonammakkal, "The Theology of Divine Names in the Genuine Works of Ephraem," (D. Phil. thesis presented to the University of Oxford, Oxford, 1991), esp. pp. 23-40. See also Thomas Koonammakkal, "Divine Names and Theological Language in Ephrem," in E.A. Livingstone (ed.), *Studia Patristica* (vol. XXV; Leuven: Peeters, 1993), pp. 318-23; idem, "The Self-Revealing God and Man in Ephrem," *The Harp* 6 (1993), pp. 233-48.

[85] Koonammakkal, "The Self-Revealing God," pp. 237 & 240.

[86] Beck, *Hymnen de Fide*, XXXI:1-2. The English translation is from Brock, *The Luminous Eye*, p. 60. For a full discussion of Ephraem's theology of the 'divine names' see Koonammakkal, "The Theology of Divine Names in the Genuine Works of Ephraem."

[87] Beck, *Hymnen de Fide*, VI:17. For a discussion of the full range of 'bridge' imagery in Ephraem's writing see Edmund Beck, "Zwei ephrämische Bilder," *Oriens Christianus* 71 (1987), pp. 1-9.

[88] J. Overbeck, *S. Ephraemi Syri Rabulae Episcopi Edesseni Balaei Aliorumque Opera Selecta* (Oxford, 1865), p. 25. English translation slightly adapted from Mitchell, *S. Ephraim's Prose Refutations*, vol. I, p. iv. See also Edmund Beck,

"Ephraems Brief an Hypatios; übersetzt und erklärt," *Oriens Christianus* 58 (1974), p. 85, n. 22 and p. 95, n. 60, for discussion of *tarʿîtâ* in Ephraem's works.

[89] Beck, *Hymnen de Paradiso*, IX:20. The English translation is adapted from Brock, *St. Ephrem the Syrian; Hymns on Paradise*, p. 143. Brock here translates *tarʿîtâ* as 'spirit.' I have chosen to use the word 'mind' as more communicative of the sense.

[90] Edmund Beck, *Des heiligen Ephraem des Syrers Hymnen de Nativitate (Epiphania)* (CSCO, vols. 186 & 187), III:4. See also the English translation of K. McVey, *Ephrem the Syrian: Hymns*, p. 83.

[91] See Edmund Beck, *Ephräms des Syrers Psychologie und Erkenntnislehre* (CSCO, vol. 419; Louvain: Peeters, 1980).

[92] See Edmund Beck, "Das Bild vom Spiegel bei Ephräm," *Orientalia Christiana Periodica* 19 (1953), pp. 5-24, esp. 5-10.

[93] Beck, *Hymnen de Fide*, LXVII:8-9. 1 Cor. 13:12 cannot be far behind Ephraem's use of the image of the mirror in this and other contexts.

[94] Beck, *Hymnen de Virginitate*, XX:12. See also the English translation in McVey, *Ephrem the Syrian: Hymns*, pp. 348-49.

[95] Edmund Beck, *Des heiligen Ephraem des Syrers Paschahymnen; (de Azymis, de Crucifixione, de Resurrectione)* (CSCO, vols. 248 & 249; Louvain: Peeters, 1964), De Azymis, IV:22-24.

[96] Beck, *Hymnen de Fide*, XLIV:1-3.

[97] See Tanios Bou Mansour, *La pensée symbolique de saint Ephrem le syrien* (Bibliothèque de l'Université Saint-Esprit, 16; Kaslik, 1988).

[98] Sebastian Brock, for example, says, "If a label is required, 'symbolic theology' would be the least inappropriate designation of Ephrem's approach. The freedom of this kind of theology from Greek modes of thought is striking." Sebastian Brock, "The Poet as Theologian," *Sobornost* 7 (1977), pp. 243-44. See also Edmund Beck, *Ephräms Trinitätslehre im Bild von Sonne/Feuer, Licht und Wärme* (CSCO, vol. 425; Louvain: Peeters, 1981).

[99] For a discussion of the definitions of these terms in Ephraem's Syriac usage, see Mansour, *La pensée symbolique*, pp. 23-71; Koonammakkal, "The Theology of Divine Names," esp. pp. 78-291.

[100] See Leloir, *Doctrines et Méthodes*, pp. 40-41; Hidal, *Interpretatio Syriaca*, p. 56. Robert Murray says, "Doch stellt seine exegetische Haltung vielleicht die schönste Ausprägung der antiochenischen Richtung dar." R. Murray, "Der Dichter als Exeget: der hl. Ephräm und die heutige Exegese," *Zeitschrift für katholische Theologie* 100 (1978), p. 486.

[101] David D. Bundy, "Language and the Knowledge of God in Ephrem Syrus," *The Patristic and Byzantine Review* 5 (1986), p. 98.

[102] Beck, *Paschahymnen*, de Azymis, III:1, ʿunîtâ.

[103] See Edmund Beck, "Symbolum-Mysterium bei Aphraat und Ephräm," *Oriens Christianus* 42 (1958), pp. 19-40; idem, "Zur Terminologie von Ephräms Bildtheologie," in Schmidt (ed.), *Typus, Symbol, Allegorie*, pp. 239-77; Georges Saber, "La typologie sacramentaire et baptismale de saint Éphrem," *Parole de l'Orient* 4 (1973), pp. 73-19; Robert Murray, "The Theory of Symbolism in St. Ephrem's Theology," *Parole de l'Orient* 6 & 7 (1975-1976), pp. 1-20; idem, "Der Dichter als Exeget," pp. 484-94; Mansour, *La pensée symbolique*, pp.26-35.

[104] See S. H. Griffith, "The Image of the Image Maker in the Poetry of St. Ephraem the Syrian," in E. A. Livingstone (ed.), *Studia Patristica* (vol. XXV; Leuven: Peeters, 1993), pp. 258-69.

[105] Beck, *Paschahymnen*, de Crucifixione, II:5.

[106] Beck, *Hymnen de Virginitate*, XXVIII:2-3. See McVey, *Ephrem the Syrian; Hymns*, p. 386.

[107] See Bertrand de Margerie, *An Introduction to the History of Exegesis* (vol. I, "The Greek Fathers," trans. L. Maluf; Petersham, MA: St. Bede's Publications, 1993), pp. 143-63,

where the author develops four 'laws' or principles to summarize Ephraem's exegetical method.

[108] Leloir, *Saint Éphrem: commentaire de l'évangile concordant; folios additionnels*, pp. 106-07. English translation from McCarthy, *Saint Ephrem's Commentary*, p. 139.

[109] Tonneau, *Sancti Ephraem Syri in Genesim*, p. 118. English translation from Mathews & Amar, *St. Ephrem the Syrian; Selected Prose Works*, p. 209. See also Hidal, *Interpretatio Syriaca*, pp. 56-60.

[110] Tonneau, *Sancti Ephraem Syri in Genesim*, p. 84. English translation from Mathews & Amar, *St. Ephrem the Syrian; Selected Prose Works*, p. 169.

[111] See Leloir, *Commentaire de l'Évangile concordant*, p. 369; McCarthy, *Saint Ephrem's Commentary*, p. 313. This passage is preserved only in the Armenian version.

[112] Leloir, *Saint Ephrem: commentaire (version arménienne)*, I:1; *idem, Commentaire de l'Évangile concordant*, p. 42. English translation from McCarthy, *Saint Ephrem's Commentary*, p. 40.

[113] Edmund Beck, *Des heiligen Ephraem des Syrers Sermones de Fide* (CSCO, vols. 212 & 213; Louvain: Peeters, 1961), II:485-92. On this theme in Ephraem's works see E. Beck, "Glaube und Gebet bei Ephräm," *Oriens Christianus* 66 (1982), pp. 15-50.

[114] Beck, *Hymnen de Fide*, LXXX:2-3.

[115] See Edmund Beck, *Des heiligen Ephraem des Syrers Hymnen de Nativitate (Epiphania)* (CSCO, vols. 186 & 187; Louvain: Peeters, 1959), VIII:17 & XIII:14. See also Griffitn, "Asceticism in the Church of Syria," pp. 223-29.

The Père Marquette Lectures in Theology

1969 *The Authority for Authority*
        Quentin Quesnell
        Professor of Theology
        Marquette University

1970 *Mystery and Truth*
        John Macquarrie
        Professor of Theology
        Union Theological Seminary

1971 *Doctrinal Pluralism*
        Bernard Lonergan, S.J.
        Professor of Theology
        Regis College, Ontario

1972 *Infallibility*
        George A. Lindbeck
        Professor of Theology
        Yale University

1973 *Ambiguity in Moral Choice*
        Richard A. McCormick, S.J.
        Professor of Moral Theology
        Bellarmine School of Theology

1974 *Church Membership as a Catholic and Ecumenical Problem*
        Avery Dulles, S.J.
        Professor of Theology
        Woodstock College

1975 *The Contributions of Theology to Medical Ethics*
      James Gustafson
      University Professor of Theological Ethics
      University of Chicago

1976 *Religious Values in an Age of Violence*
      Rabbi Marc Tannenbaum
      Director of National Interreligious Affairs
      American Jewish Committee, New York City

1977 *Truth Beyond Relativism:*
     Karl Mannheim's Sociology of Knowledge
      Gregory Baum
      Professor of Theology and Religious Studies
      St. Michael's College

1978 *A Theology of 'Uncreated Energies'*
      George A. Maloney, S.J.
      Professor of Theology
      John XXIII Center for Eastern Christian
      Studies
      Fordham University

1980 *Method in Theology:*
     An Organon For Our Time
      Frederick E. Crowe, S.J.
      Research Professor in Theology
      Regis College, Toronto

1981 *Catholics in the Promised Land of the Saints*
      James Hennesey, S.J.
      Professor of the History of Christianity
      Boston College

1982 *Whose Experience Counts in Theological Reflection?*
    Monika Hellwig
    Professor of Theology
    Georgetown University

1983 *The Theology and Setting of Discipleship in the
Gospel of Mark*
    John R. Donahue, S.J.
    Professor of Theology
    Jesuit School of Theology, Berkeley

1984 *Should War be Eliminated? Philosophical and
Theological Investigations*
    Stanley Hauerwas
    Professor of Theology
    Notre Dame University

1985 *From Vision to Legislation:
From the Council to a Code of Laws*
    Ladislas M. Orsy, S.J.
    Professor of Canon Law
    The Catholic University of America

1986 *Revelation and Violence:
A Study in Contextualization*
    Walter Brueggemann
    Professor of Old Testament
    Eden Theological Seminary
    St. Louis, Missouri

1987 *Nova et Vetera:*
The Theology of Tradition in American Catholicism
        Gerald Fogarty
        Professor of Religious Studies
        University of Virginia

1988 *The Christian Understanding of Freedom and the*
History of Freedom in the Modern Era:
The Meeting and Confrontation Between
Christianity and the Modern Era in a Postmodern
Situation
        Walter Kasper
        Professor of Dogmatic Theology
        University of Tübingen

1989 *Moral Absolutes: Catholic Tradition, Current*
Trends, and the Truth
        William F. May
        Ordinary Professor of Moral Theology
        Catholic University of America

1990 *Is Mark's Gospel a Life of Jesus? The Question of*
Genre
        Adela Yarbro Collins
        Professor of New Testament
        University of Notre Dame

1991 *Faith, History and Cultures:*
Stability and Change in Church Teachings
        Walter H. Principe, C.S.B.
        Professor of Theology
        University of Toronto

1992 *Universe and Creed*
      Stanley L. Jaki
      Distinguished University Professor
      Seton Hall University

1993 *The Resurrection of Jesus Christ:*
Some Contemporary Issues
      Gerald G. O'Collins, S.J.
      University Professor
      Gregorian Pontifical University

1994 *Seeking God in Contemporary Culture*
      Most Reverend Rembert G. Weakland, O.S.B.
      Archbishop of Milwaukee

1995 *The Book of Proverbs and Our Search for Wisdom*
      Richard J. Clifford, S.J.
      Weston Jesuit School of Theology

1996 *Orthodox and Catholic Sister Churches: East is West*
      and West is East
      Michael A. Fahey, S.J.
      University of St. Michael's College, Toronto

1997 *'Faith Adoring the Mystery': Reading the Bible with*
St. Ephraem the Syrian
      Sidney H. Griffith
      Catholic University of America

About the Père Marquette Lecture Series

The Annual Père Marquette Lecture Series began at Marquette University in the Spring of 1969. Ideal for classroom use, library additions, or private collections, the Père Marquette Lecture Series has received international acceptance by scholars, universities, and libraries. Hardbound in blue cloth with gold stamped covers. Uniform style and price ($15 each). Some reprints with soft covers. Complete set (26 Titles) receives a 40% discount. New standing orders receive a 30% discount. Regular reprinting keeps all volumes available. Ordering information (purchase orders, checks, and major credit cards accepted):

Bookmasters Distribution Services
P.O. Box 388
1444 U.S. Route 42
Ashland OH 44805
Order Toll-Free (800) 247-6553
FAX: (419) 281 6883

Editorial Address:
Dr. Andrew Tallon, Director
Marquette University Press
Box 1881
Milwaukee WI 53201-1881
Tel: (414) 288-7298
FAX: (414) 288-3300
Internet: tallona@vms.csd.mu.edu
CompuServe : 73627,1125.

ISBN 0-87462-577-7

9 780874 625776